RED-EYED TREE FROG

Story by

Joy Cowley

Illustrated with photographs by

Nic Bishop

SCHOLASTIC INC.

New York Toronto London Auckland Sydney
Mexico City New Delhi Hong Kong Buenos Aires

Evening comes to the rain forest.

The macaw
and the toucan
will soon go to sleep.

But the red-eyed tree frog
has been asleep all day.

It wakes up hungry.
What will it eat?

Here is an iguana.
Frogs do not eat iguanas.

Do iguanas eat frogs?
The red-eyed tree frog
does not wait to find out.

It hops onto
another branch.

The frog is hungry
but it will not eat the ant.

It will not eat
the katydid.

Will it eat the caterpillar?

No!
The caterpillar is poisonous.

Something moves near the frog.

Something slips and slithers along a branch.
It is a hungry boa snake.

The snake flicks its tongue.
It tastes frog in the air.
Look out, frog!

JUMP!

The frog lands on a leaf,
far away from the boa.

What does the frog
see on the leaf?

A moth!

Crunch, crunch, crunch!

The tree frog is
no longer hungry.

It climbs
onto a leaf.

The red-eyed tree frog shuts its eyes . . .

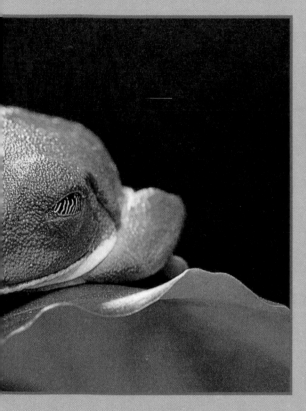

and goes to sleep . . .

ISBN 0-439-78221-X

Text copyright © 1999 by Joy Cowley.
Photographs copyright © 1999 by Nic Bishop.

12 11 10 9 8 7 6 5 4 3   6 7 8 9 10 11/0

Printed in the U.S.A.   40

First Bookshelf edition, March 2006

Book design by David Caplan.
The text type was set in 27-point Myriad 565 Condensed.

The photographer used original high-speed photographic techniques to capture the images that appear in this book.

Cover photographs © 1999 by Nic Bishop.